TAKING YOUR COMPANY
PUBLIC

A CORPORATE STRATEGIES MANUAL

JAMES SCOTT

A New Renaissance Corporation publication
First Edition

ISBN: 0-9891467-0-7
ISBN: 978-0-9891467-0-8

Publisher:
New Renaissance Corporation
73 Old Dublin Pike, Suite 10 # 142
Doylestown, PA 18901
www.newrenaissancecorporation.com

DISCLAIMER AND/OR LEGAL NOTICES
The information presented herein represents the views of the author as of the date of publication. Because of the rate with which conditions change, the author reserves the rights to alter and update their opinions based on the new conditions.

The author has strived to be as accurate and complete as possible in the creation of this report, notwithstanding the fact that she does not warrant or represent at any time that the contents within are accurate due to the rapidly changing nature of the Internet.

While all attempts have been made to verify information provided in this publication, the author assumes no responsibility for errors, omissions, or contrary interpretation of the subject matter herein. Any perceived slights of specific persons, peoples, or organizations are unintentional.

TABLE OF CONTENTS

It's More Than Just Taking Your Company Public
Globalizing Your Company - It's you Against the Machine
Take a Company Public? You're a Tasty Treat for Wolves
Hiring a Corporate Attorney

Corporate Structuring Process
    1. C-Level Evaluation
    2. BOD Evaluation
    3. Strategic Alliances
    4. Strategic Business Plan
    5. PPM to Sell Equity Legally
Viral Publicity Campaign
    1. Encompass the Corporation
    2. Publicize each Executive

Plug-in Business Models

Controlling Movement Is the Beginning of Controlling the Mind

Carry a Big Stick? No, Carry a Steel Club!

Corporate Strategies: Chaos With an Agenda

Crisis Consultants

The Road to Public Markets

PREFACE

This book deals with the process of taking a company public, from forming the initial public offering to beginning operations. Entrepreneurs who are pressed for time often find this process difficult due to its many steps. Most books on this subject fail to offer first-hand, practical advice on taking a company public, whereas this book is intended to provide definitive guidance.

Taking a company public is every entrepreneur's dream, and it also offers major financial rewards, prestige and glamour. It is also a complex process that often intimidates entrepreneurs, and requires specialists in many disciplines such as accountants, attorneys, consultants and public relations executives. These professionals may possess a thorough knowledge of their area of expertise, but they rarely have a total grasp of the entire process of taking a company public. This book fulfills the need of the Chief Executive Officer and the IPO team to obtain a more complete understanding of this complex subject.

HOW TO USE THIS BOOK

Think of this book as a situation handbook for companies that are going public or expanding. This manual offers step-by-step formulas for topics such as going public, investor relations, globalizing a concept, troubleshooting underperforming stock, corporate structuring and much more. It provides strategy templates for the most common occurrences of going public. The reader will find a complete solution under one easy-to-find heading for each situation that arises.

Industry gurus who charge top dollar for their consulting services have used these procedures, and they can work miracles for your business when applied properly. We have made every effort to make most current and compliant methods available, although local, state and federal statutes and regulations are ever-changing and evolving. Check with your legal counsel before implementing these or other concepts into your business model.

ABOUT THE AUTHOR

James Scott is a consultant, author and lecturer on the topics of IPO facilitation, corporate structuring, Private Placement Memorandum authoring and Mergers and Acquisitions strategies. Mr. Scott has authored multiple books such as 'The Book on Mergers and Acquisitions', 'Taking Your Company Public', 'The Book on PPMs: Regulation D 504 Edition', 'The Book on PPMs: Regulation D 505 Edition', 'The Book on PPMs: Regulation D 506 Edition' as well as several templates that make the process of completing complicated S1 and PPM docs as easy as 'point and click' for entrepreneurs and corporate CEOs.

Mr. Scott is a member of several economic think tanks that study diverse aspects of legislation concepts that effect corporations worldwide such as: Aspen Institute, Chatham House: Royal Institute of International Affairs, The American Enterprise Institute, Economic Research Council, American Institute for Economic Research, The Manhattan Institute and The Hudson Institute among others.

To contact James Scott visit the 'Contact Us' page at the New Renaissance Corporation publishing website at: www.newrenaissancecorporation.com

CHAPTER 1

CAN YOU GO PUBLIC?

Companies may go public for many different reasons such as expansion, the need for capital, exit strategy, acquisition facilitation and globalization. What are the real advantages to going public?

Let's go over the disadvantages first. Your life becomes an open book as an executive of a public company. Your spending habits and failures will be a matter of public information along with your annual and quarterly filings. You'll also be accountable to shareholders. You'll have a board whose main interest is the company and the shareholders. The board members will not be interested in you or your need for a new luxury car, financial bonus or a quick loan from the company. These things were easy to obtain when your company was a sole proprietor entity. You need to maintain trading volume since your stock is worthless without it, and will make your company blind, deaf, mute and quadriplegic. This view is a bit extreme but you get the point.

The advantages of taking your company public are numerous. This requires you to maintain a solid trading volume, minimal dilution of stock, solid executive management, an active board of directors, powerful strategic alliances and the ongoing advice of a strategies consultant. Your company can expand through acquisition, subsidiary mergers, and the purchase of entities and services with stock to retain cash flow. Banks and other institutional lenders can also make more funding solutions available. These steps will provide you with a built-in, turn-key exit strategy.

The most successful public companies have a few common themes built into their infrastructure. They have recruited a proven and tested CEO, CFO and COO with professional pedigrees and track records. These personnel should also be recognized in the industry and bring a strong following of partners and solution mechanisms with them. This strategy will typically yield instantaneous, empirical results on behalf of the company. The board of directors should also be restructured so they represent major industry-enhancing components such as the legal, financial, distribution, domestic and international industry niches. Each of these board members should put their contact portfolio to work to achieve immediate, long-term growth and stabilization for your company.

If my Company goes public, I'll hire a COO!

Another aspect that all prosperous public entities have is a strategies consultant, commonly known as a fixer, who keeps everything in line. This professional will typically stand in the background, constantly analyzing every aspect of the company for weak points and correcting them. A fixer typically has a keen eye and a massive contact base that can correct virtually any situation quickly and seamlessly when put into place. This strategist often fixes problems such as a lazy board member, potential acquisition, a CEO who is not pulling his or her weight and potential legal issues.

Going public is a great strategy for the right organization. Having all your ducks in a row before and after going public is the key to a successful and long-lived offering.

CHAPTER 2

SETTING UP A CORPORATE STRUCTURE

The same rules apply when setting up a company structure that is conducive to globalization, scalability, attracting the right alliances and service contracts whether you are a private, public or pre-IPO corporation.

You'll need a solid CEO, CFO and a COO, depending on the size of your company. The company founder often needs to step back and let a professional, well-pedigreed CEO take control of the expansion. Don't allow your company to become another cautionary tale. A founder who is full of pride and has a limited pedigree will absolutely take his or her company down. Which is more important, your company or stimulating your ego? Throw in the towel now if your ego comes first, because you'll never make it in today's tumultuous economic environment.

Selecting a CEO can be difficult considering the skill sets that a qualified individual must have. The most important criterion is a proven track record for success, followed by the CEO's contact portfolio that he or she is bringing into your company. This portfolio will provide your company with expedient growth opportunities via strategic alliance possibilities, political and legislative contacts, established inter-industry vendors, executives and the ability to raise funds. Perform a Google search on your CEO candidates and hire an investigator run a background check. Ensure the candidates have solid credit scores as this is a strong indicator of how they will manage your company. They'll be reckless in person if they look reckless on paper. Do the same thing for the CFO candidates but also ensure they have experience with forensic accounting, Forms 10-K and 10-Q, annual and ongoing internal auditing.

Put your board of directors together once your executive lineup is in place. The pedigree of the executive lineup will dictate the type of board members you attract. Always pick an odd number of members to avoid stalemates when critical issues come to a vote. The board members' expertise should cover legal, financial and industry areas at a minimum. Small and medium-size companies typically have five board members. Allow room for funding sources such as venture capital, private equity and large angel investors who want a board position in order to manage their investments.

Board member compensation is typically a combination of restricted stock and exercisable options. Each member must go through the same qualification process as the C-level executives, and you should also hold them to the confines of a solid contract that defines their position in detail. Leave nothing to subjective interpretation.

Place an advisory board under your board of directors. This group is similar to the BOD in some ways but very different in others. AB members are typically professionals who are actively attempting to increase their professional pedigrees to eventually qualify as a full-fledged BOD member. These professionals will typically receive compensation with restricted stock and provide support when issues requiring their particular skill set arise. AB members are often the workhorses of the company because they provide free services for the BOD members who are setting up internal expansion or audit groups.

The next step in establishing the corporate structure is to reach out to complementary entities for strategic alliances. These companies or individuals will enter into a mutually beneficial relationship for co-op advertising, collective contract negotiation, contact sharing, BOD and AB sharing, and the liberal referral of sources and clients. Strategic alliances are often specified as contractual obligations for board members, advisory board members and C-level executives. These alliances should also carry over to general employee tasks as well, including weekly or quarterly meetings. It is crucial that new strategic alliances are identified and facilitated.

Small and mid-sized companies often overlook the importance of the legislative side of business, but large corporations always have this in place. You'll probably need a corporate strategies consultant to put this piece together as it requires a specialized skill set and must be done properly for optimal affect.

Your goal here is not to meet the figurehead of a political interest such as a senator or member of Congress. You must instead get to the root of the power. You'll need to get on the side of the political lobby, special interest group or individual whose funds and influence dictate the outcome of the figurehead's election. These are the true keys to the political kingdom. The politician is the individual who puts a face to the cause of these organizations and supports the issues that he is guided to enforce.

These are just a few of the mandatory prerequisites of creating a solid foundation for a company that is built to last.

Several other intricacies to the formula exist, but the above steps generally provide a solid point of entry.

IT'S MORE THAN JUST TAKING YOUR COMPANY PUBLIC

Here is what your company will look like after a Princeton Corporate Solutions Overhaul

Client Company After – Princeton Corporate Solutions Strategy Facilitation

Board of directors selection

Board of advisors selection

C-level executive selection and qualification

Strategic alliance identification and facilitation

Pre-public expansion strategy identification and facilitation

Business plan authoring

Private placement memorandum authoring (if needed)

Investor referral program

Third party audit

S1 filing and comments by our legal teams

15c211 filing by our market maker selection, FINRA trading symbol achieved

Powerful post-public investor relations solutions by partner companies to create market and build stock value and trading volume

Corporate and product/service publicity using TV and radio panel interviews to promote the knowledge of executive, build corporate brand and get trading symbol out to the masses.

Post-public acquisition identification and facilitation solutions

Post-public subsidiary mergers and acquisition identification and solutions

GLOBALIZING YOUR COMPANY - IT'S YOU AGAINST THE MACHINE

A system is in place for globalization which you need to become part of in order to expand. There is no organized group of puppeteers controlling your economic fate, and there is a solution for any obstacle in your path. Economics and international expansionism combine formula and contacts.

The formula portion of this equation is the process of establishing corporate structure and strategic organization. The contact part comes into effect by putting that corporate structure and strategy in place. This sounds like an illogical spewing of pointless doubletalk, but let me explain. The formula for globalizing your company consists of the following:

BOD and advisory board recruitment and qualification

CEO, CFO and COO recruitment

Strategic alliance build-out

Pre-public valuation, modest fundraising, third-party audit (PCAOB), S1 filing, 15c211 Filing

Trading Symbol issued, investor relations

Growth and globalization funded via monetized public securities

The use of contacts is the second part of this process. The key people in your company need to collectively gather their contacts and put them to work. Board members, advisers and C-level executives need to pin a map to the wall and place tacks in the geographic locations where you have contacts. Split up the map and begin setting up strategic alliances for distribution, legal representation, legislative contacts and promotional partners. The objective here is to create small structures throughout these locations in a strategic manner that is synergetic to both your contacts and your team members.

The company founders who will be responsible for putting this plan in motion should find a consultant who specializes in strategic planning, globalization and IPO facilitation. This person will guide you through the process. These consultants are expensive but worth their weight in gold since they will help you recruit executives, board members and advisers with the proper pedigree. They will also form initial strategic alliances in a straightforward and expedient manner. Why reinvent the wheel and complicate things? An amateur entering into this world is like a baby trying to dogpaddle across a shark tank. It's just a matter of time until the predator sniffs out the prey and then all bets are off. Globalize your product, service or franchise opportunity quickly and easily with the proper team, structure, formula and contacts.

TAKE A COMPANY PUBLIC? YOU'RE A TASTY TREAT FOR WOLVES

Many companies make gargantuan mistakes that are irreversible when it comes to fundraising. You need to know that you are a tantalizing snack for industry wolves, whether you're taking a company public, finding an attorney to file your S1 form or using a consultant to write a private placement memorandum to raise capital.

Companies seeking these services with ill-informed executive decision makers often fall prey to predatory consultants who have no intention of fulfilling the services for which they are being hired, and couldn't do if they wanted to. Upstarts and fast talkers who call themselves business consultants may be nothing more than resellers of a service provider who is a boilerplate, template-driven organization that lacks the contacts or know-how to facilitate an IPO, S1 or PPM.

You'll be pulled in by their promise of delivery, mechanical jargon, grasp of the technical intricacies and polished use of terminology. But buyer beware! Nine out of every ten consultants that I've come across don't know the difference between a reverse merger, Regulation D Rule 504 and Regulation D Rule 506. Even worse, new or wannabe S1 facilitators often confuse a DPO with an IPO. The client, who doesn't know what questions to ask, is left with a structure he or she can't capitalize.

I received a request from an organization that wanted to go public at a time when my schedule was completely booked. I referred the transaction, writing an IPO for the potential client, to a lawyer whose office was near the client and who had been calling me for months to get a project. I soon saw the PPM she authored and it was all wrong. She had convinced the client to go with a DPO instead of an IPO. A DPO requires dealing with state regulators and wasn't the right fit for the company. I should have checked out the lawyer's knowledge before I referred her.

Stay away from pushy sales-oriented organizations if you're looking for a real consultant who can actually come through with solutions for expansion strategies. It's better to hire a consultant whom you have to call three times to get through on the phone and then tries to talk you out of moving forward. This consultant is testing you and your dedication to your company and project. The best consultants start out with, "OK, tell me about your business and what are you trying to accomplish?" They'll ask about your C-level executives, investor exit strategy, product and service intricacies, marketing plan, three-year projections, strategic alliances in place, board of directors and more. Your response to these questions will help the strategist make a plan to set up a structure that works.

Stay away from broker types who claim to love your business and don't poke holes in your corporate structure, expansion strategy, board of directors or other elements of your business. Walk away from those who try to disguise their true lack of comprehension with technical jargon. They are just trying to distract you from the fact that they don't have a clue as to what they are doing. There are also many other distraction techniques.

Watch out for services that simply author business plans and PPMs without running through your exit strategy scenarios. I'm sorry to be the bearer of bad news, but accredited investors are not impressed with quarterly and annual dividends. They want to know when they will get their money back, as well as the risk and the return on their investment. General authoring services will typically have no ability to form strategies and they almost always work from templates.

Use a service provider that can take you from point A to point B in-house or with a solid team that is outsourced according to specialty. The service provider should also have a lead consultant who remains the "head coach" and conducts the process all the way through. Keep them accountable and don't set yourself up to be the monkey in the middle of a "pass the blame" game.

HIRING A CORPORATE ATTORNEY

A frustrating misconception exists that is rampant among entrepreneurs. The notion that you should hire an attorney based on rate or claimed expertise is beyond ludicrous and absolutely laughable. Attorneys just throw technical jargon at you, look down their nose at you and name their rate. You'll pay it just like a chump because after all, who are you to argue? This chapter will tell you exactly who you are when talking to an attorney for services.

Retain your attorney before you are in a crunch. As a business owner, you'll most likely go to a contracts attorney to get your paperwork reviewed for loopholes and verbiage. Obtain referrals from friends and colleagues, and compile a list of candidates. Make a list of questions that you're going to go over with them. The theme and timing of the questions are important to achieve an optimal effect.

Establish a playing field. Attorneys are accustomed to running the conversation and the last thing that they are expecting is for the client to actually have a solid grasp of what they want. Read over their biographies on their website and look over any groundbreaking cases in which they played a key role in securing a victory on behalf of the client. If they aren't litigators, examine their history of publishing case law concepts and other identifiers of expert status such as TV, radio or podcast interviews.

Do they sit on the board of any prestigious organizations? What have they done to add exclamation marks to their law niches and what makes them the latest and greatest the industry has to offer? What makes an attorney the best choice for you? Walk out if he doesn't seem willing to step up and sell himself. Don't waste another second in that office. You'll regret hiring this attorney when it's time to use his services because he will fail.

Continue with the inquisition if the candidate answers promptly and you like what you hear. Attorneys usually love to talk about themselves, so get them to talk about the types of industries they serve. The key is to determine the type of client base they have. This part is important since you're going to ask them about client retention and what they do to enhance the corporations in their client base.

I'm talking about strategic alliances. You should expect introductions to his client base for mutually beneficial and profitable relationships if your attorney truly serves all those companies and has been in the industry for many years. One thing I know about attorneys who deal with businesses is that the bad ones only want to hear from you when you have a problem or crisis because then they get to charge top dollar and they don't have to do anything but file paperwork or make a couple of calls and hold on to the rest of the retainer.

Good attorneys will maintain communication with you during the good and bad times. They will also make introductions and help you get to that next level so they can start charging you premiums. Nothing is wrong with that because good attorneys are worth their weight in gold, and you'll be able to avoid making bad decisions that lead to legal issues by keeping up good communication.

Your lawyer should provide a lot more than just legal navigation, and should act like a referral hub on steroids. Demand that type of service from your corporate attorney and accept nothing less. Your attorney will be lazy during bad times if he or she is lazy during good times, and you'll be the one to suffer. You don't want a calm, laid-back attorney. He or she should be cool and collected under pressure, but constantly spouting off introductions and strategic partnership opportunities. Never hire an attorney without these qualities in mind.

CHAPTER 3

THE STEP-BY-STEP PROCESS IN PLAIN ENGLISH

Here are some basic things you need to know if you're looking to get your company public and listed on the OTCBB, NYSE and NASDAQ.

CORPORATE STRUCTURING PROCESS

1. C-Level Evaluation

You'll need to do some corporate structuring. Your C-level executives must have decent educational and professional pedigrees so they can pass due diligence.

2. BOD Evaluation

Elect a BOD if you haven't already done so, and evaluate them. Each member of the board should have something

solid to offer in the form of strategic alliances, financing contacts or other key elements the business needs.

3. Strategic Alliances

Structure strategic alliances with other companies and bring
them in to peg your business model so you can increase your
distribution. You can then capitalize on their publicity and
team up on various ventures.

4. Strategic Business Plan

Next is to put together a strategic business plan that breaks
your intentions down into steps and includes any financials
you might have. For financial projections, go out about three
years. This is sufficient for private investors and private equity funds you're seeking in your pre-IPOs.

5. PPM to Sell Equity Legally

Break down the amount your company needs to raise, and
divide it into shares. Create a PPM using these figures to
help you sell equity in your company while complying with
SEC guidelines.

VIRAL PUBLICITY CAMPAIGN

Create a streamlined publicity campaign once your structure is in place. You should design it to go viral on the Internet by spreading your campaign throughout various social
networks.

1. Encompass the Corporation

The campaign for publicity should focus on the corporation by emphasizing the company name and its industry. Conduct individual campaigns on specific products and services.

2. Publicize each Executive

A publicity campaign that wraps around each executive demonstrates to the public, potential investors, contacts and alliances that these executives are indeed authorities in their specific fields of expertise.

Viral publicity can be broken down into five major genres:

- Videos - High-visibility video sites such as YouTube.

- Social and News Bookmarks

- Unique Articles - Articles written by executives of the company provide a great way to raise their profiles and show leadership within the industry.

- Press Releases - These brief announcements are great outlets for talking about what your individual executives and your company is doing as well as announcing new projects, products and services.

- Podcasts - You should strip the audio content from your videos and place them into podcasts. You should also consider hiring a voiceover specialist to read your articles and press releases, and place these recordings into podcasts.

FIND A CORPORATE CONSULTANT

Find a solid corporate consultant.

A corporate strategies consultant should specialize in getting companies ready to go public. He or she should also package the company in a way that's conducive to raising capital in a steady, streamlined and rapid manner.

A consultant should provide:

- Attorneys to file an S1. Good attorneys should be able to go to the comments stage and wrap everything up within 3 to 4 months.

- SEC-approved auditors. They are also known as third-party peer review or peek-a-boo auditors. You'll also need a PCAOB auditor for the OTCBB.

- Market makers to file the 15c211 with FINRA.

- Investor relations contacts for the post-public campaign to strengthen your stock position and price. This strategy will preserve both the short-term and long-term results of your share price.

- Publicist contacts. These consultants should have several publicist contacts who deal with different types of media such as newspapers and industry-specific journals. They should also be able to get you on expert panels, and set up radio and TV interviews.

CHAPTER 4

BECOME A CEO WHO CAN MAKE A DIFFERENCE

THINGS TO DO

Here's a quick list of things to do to become an expert in your field. This will allow you to grow your professional pedigree and make a name for yourself.

Select an industry niche.

Submerse yourself in that industry and get to know all the players. Read all the books, magazines, articles and press releases. Learn everything you can about that industry.

Get involved at every level.

Join the top 20 industry special interest groups such as your industry's version of the chamber of commerce. Volunteer for projects and tasks, and get elected to boards and committees. Update the group's email list, head up projects and do anything else you can think of to increase your involvement with that group.

Post articles about your industry.

Gather all of your information about the industry, especially current events. Write articles that are both fact-based and opinion-based to post on your blog or personal website. Your blog and website should feature your resume to generate traffic. You'll create a following of regular readers with frequently changing information that reflects good insight, which will lead to invitations to become involved in industry groups.

Submit how-to videos demonstrating your expert capabilities.

Create videos about specific topics within your industry that provide good, solid advice to demonstrate your expert status. Base the video on a PowerPoint presentation with a Camtasia voiceover. You can show these videos on your blog and at speaking engagements.

Create press releases about you and new projects.

Issue a solid, well-written press release about every activity you get involved in within your industry. Attach a picture of yourself and everyone with whom you're working. Most press release sites allow this practice.

Make yourself available for expert panel participation.

This will allow you to discuss areas of interest within your industry. These panels will help spread your name and personal brand to an interested population by using handouts for the audience. The media and industry organizations will eventually begin calling and that's when the magic happens.

Get on BODs and advisory boards.

Seek opportunities to get appointed to BODs and advisory boards for any organizations by using your contacts in industry groups, the media and your blog. Board members often receive stock options such as restricted stock. These titles are also great for building your resume since they reinforce your expertise and leadership.

Getting Attention From Executive Recruiters

The busier you are the more executive recruiters will want you to fill board and executive positions. It's human nature to want what we can't or don't have. An executive who's available and eager is a less desirable marketable asset than one who has published work, sprinkled how-to videos on the Internet and is intricately involved with the upper echelon powerbase within your industry niche. The greater your visibility, the higher your reputation as a key expert will be.

Continue to raise your profile by getting your articles published in industry journals and the local newspaper. Make yourself available to television and radio news programs as an industry expert. Consult for free with industry blogs and websites with high traffic that provide public relations value. Work out a publicity deal in exchange for your efforts.

You'll begin to get opportunities to serve on BODs for public companies after you've proven yourself an active adviser, and your name is associated with successful transactions. You'll typically begin with the OTCBB and eventually join the NASDAQ and NYSE.

Open up the floodgates and let the offers come rolling in once you've established a pedigree. You'll need to demonstrate an empirical evidence of strategy, contacts and the ability to work with a board for the short-term and long-term betterment of the company,

BECOMING THE EXECUTIVE YOU WANT TO BE

Many professionals, entrepreneurs and business owners are a far cry from where they would like to be in their current position within their company and industry. What is the factor that thrusts some people and companies forward, and why are some of them struggling behind like obsolete room-size computers in a handheld PC world?

It's actually quite simple and it all comes down to a decision to step up and dominate in a no-holds-barred, bare-knuckle fight to the finish. You need to be comfortable with the fact that not everyone will make it. Most of your colleagues and professional friends are not psychologically or professionally built to last, meaning they are not willing to do whatever it takes to get to that next level.

Decide on what you want, who you want to be and where you want to go in your career. Surround yourself with people who have the characteristics you're seeking to acquire. It will probably require several people to embody all of the characteristics you want in your future self, so find at least ten people with whom to become associated and use them as models. Don't just imitate the outward and obvious characteristics but absorb the aura of their overall presence. They may be calm and collected at times, but arrogant and rude at others. What are their hobbies and extracurricular interests? These interests are a contributing factor to whom they have become.

Overcome any obstacles that stand in your way. Dump friends and associates who are not supportive as they will only hold you back. Quickly sever ties with any and all counterproductive individuals and interests who prevent you from achieving your goal.

You should be putting on your psychological garb every morning as you're getting dressed or brushing your teeth. Slip into the mindset of that person you want to be and put blinders on your eyes so there are no distractions. You'll find that opportunities will seem to fall into your lap because you are willingly submersing yourself into a subculture. This mindset has worked for all of those around you who are living the dream of which you'll soon be a part.

You'll begin to steamroll forward as you step into this new code of conduct and professional character. Some people will be crushed under the wheel of your progress but this is a natural part of evolution. Some people dominate while others submit. Use the characteristic of arrogance as a form of self-promotion, instead of a crutch for insecurity.

State your opinion on industry-specific blogs and put out videos on viral media sites with industry information. Bring Internet surfers to your blogs and videos with social and news bookmarking links scattered all over the web. Brand yourself as the god of your industry. Your opinion matters and other people will begin to see these ideas as the norm over time. They will feel that they have been misinformed until now and view you as a person on the cutting edge of your industry with the information they need.

Don't stop whatever you do when you build momentum! You can take it one step further with articles and press releases submitted to global and high-profile directories and sites. This strategy will allow you to gain traction in growing your own personal brand and subculture within the industry. This is just the beginning but you are on your way to absolute industry domination!

CHAPTER 5

REGULATION D PRIVATE PLACEMENT MEMORANDUMS AND INVESTOR SOLICITATION

Taxpayers bailed out the banks when they went broke, so who's bailing you out of your business funding needs?

Regulation D Rules 504, 505 and 506 may come to mind. These mechanisms allow an exemption from SEC registration so that companies can raise capital via a PPM. Reg. D is a popular fundraising exemption because it allows companies to raise capital from the public such as friends and family members via private placement. Regulation D Rule 506 is commonly used because it allows fundraising above $5 million. Rule 504 allows up to $1 million and Rule 505 allows up to $5 million.

One misconception that entrepreneurs have about using Regulation D to raise capital is that they can directly solicit the public for investment capital. This is not the case, since the PPM is for insiders only and you should offer it to anyone outside of your immediate contact sphere. Failure to comply with this aspect of SEC regulation can shut down your raise before it even starts and rightfully so, since the purpose of these laws is to protect consumers and bring order to a capital raise. Worse yet, it is something your competitors will use against you down the road.

Don't be naive. When you raise capital, you're telling your competitors one of two things. You're either telling them that you're growing and need the capital to expand or you need to capital to survive. Competitors will use every angle to sucker punch you when you're down.

Look past the fact that the SEC will shut down your raise immediately upon discovering your failure to comply with regulations. Your competitors are watching you to learn about the methods you're using to raise capital, the approaches you're using for expansion, the investors to whom you're talking and the methods you're using to communicate with investors. These investors may be insiders or accredited strangers whom you are directly soliciting.

A possible example of this scenario is that the SEC receives an anonymous call just as your capital raise is winding down and you're about to start spending some of that escrow cash. You won't find out until three months down the road that the anonymous caller was that kid you fired three years ago, who is now working in the sales office of your largest competitor. Your capital is now frozen, investors are ticked off and that PCAOB audit you had set up before your S1 filing is on hold because you're under investigation. Your problems are just beginning.

Obtain funding the right way if you're using a PPM to obtain funding. Hire a professional and always get legal advice so you comply with all laws and regulations. You should also keep a lid on your source of funding. Assume you follow all the SEC rules when bringing in capital from friends and family members. Most of your competitors will drop a line to the SEC, attorney general's office and even the IRS when they find out about any alleged irregularity. This cut-throat behavior is due to these companies trying to survive in the current economy.

Your competitors may lie, but the government will still allow them to remain anonymous. You'll be presumed guilty until you can prove yourself innocent, and the false allegations will be just as damning as if you had actually taken the wrong approach.

Everyone is watching what their competitors are doing in this market. Watch your back and emphasize the importance of privacy and secrecy to potential investors. Follow the rules and keep your lips zipped. Don't let anything jeopardize your funding.

CHAPTER 6

PREPARING TO GO PUBLIC AND POST-PUBLIC INVESTOR RELATIONS POWER

CURRENT FINANCIAL STATE OF THE COMPANY

You should look at the financial state of the company, your debt, any liabilities and potential lawsuits against the company before you go public. These issues should be resolved before you begin to go public.

CORPORATE INFRASTRUCTURE

Look into your corporate infrastructure to ensure it's conducive to rapid growth and expansion. Plan for globalization by ensuring your business model includes international scalability.

C-LEVEL EXECUTIVE PEDIGREE

The executives within your company must have a proven track record of success with companies that are in your current position. People who are investing in mutual funds or post-public financing options such as a private investment in public equity are going to look at the professional track records of your executive management team.

STRATEGIC ALLIANCES

Strategic alliances are very important for increasing distribution and streamlining capacity, as is your post-public acquisition strategy.

TEAM FACILITATING THE IPO

Establish a consulting team to help you facilitate the IPO process. You'll probably miss important elements and do a less effective job if you try to make an initial public offering. Good choices for these team members typically include market makers, broker dealers, OTCBB, IPO facilitation firms, globalization consultants and strategy consultants.

PRE-PUBLIC SHARE PRICE AND ANTICIPATED IPO PRICE

Look at your pre-public share price and realistically determine your IPO price before taking your company public.

You'll have a better idea on how to do this after you start your audit and look at your corporate financial reports. You should also consult with a market maker, a corporate consultant or a strategy consultant to help you establish a share price. You really won't know what the market will bear until you actually go public, but you should have a general idea before you initiate this process.

POST-PUBLIC INVESTOR RELATIONS

Put together a post-public investor relations strategy by starting with your pre-public strategy and backing into your public strategy. Hire a professional to perform this critical task.

POST-PUBLIC ACQUISITION STRATEGY

You'll need acquisitions and mergers because you can't grow a public company organically.

WHAT IS IN AN INVESTOR RELATIONS CAMPAIGN?

Post-public investor relations are crucial. You should have a plan for informing investors of your IPO and corporate updates before going public. You should also work with an investor relations consultant or strategist during the S1 comments phase. This strategy ensures you'll be ready to go when you obtain your public offering.

YOU SHOULD CONSIDER SEVEN GENERAL ISSUES WHEN CREATING YOUR INVESTOR RELATIONS PROGRAM.

1. Corporate Publicity via Traditional Channels

You can obtain general corporate publicity through traditional channels. This generally involves getting your CEO, COO and other members of executive management on TV news, talk radio, newspaper interviews and industry periodicals. You should also attempt to get these experts on journal shows for television and radio. These talk shows should target investors, accredited investors, penny traders and global stock traders to stock exchanges such as the Frankfurt Exchange, OTCBB, NASDAQ and New York Stock Exchange.

2. Viral Publicity

You'll also need strong Internet and social network publicity. Potential investors often initiate a general Google search on the company and its principals before investing in a stock. It's essential that these searches retrieve large amounts of good information on MySpace, Facebook, how-to videos, unique article submissions and press releases. All these search results contribute to the investor's decision to invest and the investment amount. They will also determine whether investors use a buy-and-hold strategy or invest as day traders. Buy-and-hold investors are generally better, although day traders can increase the daily volume of your company's stock.

3. Press Release Announcements

Press releases to the media can announce any current event with your company from potential acquisitions, mergers, releases of various products and services, new executives and strategic partnerships. They can also cover the expansion of your company into international, regional or domestic arenas. You should announce all of these events with a press release and solid press release distribution.

4. Phone Room Market Creation Support

You'll also need a phone room to help you create the initial market for your stock. This is not a boiler room with a bunch of guys calling and selling stock. Your phone room will create the market by contacting appropriate investors, market makers and broker dealers to ensure they are aware of your stock.

Even a privately held company can have a phone room used to solicit leases, drilling partners, and property to acquire.

5. Email Alerts to an Opt-in Database

You'll probably have an opt-in email database of clients, strategic partners, and investors during the S1 phase, maybe even before you initiate your public offering. Send email alerts to these contacts constantly, and give them first crack at your press release announcements, article submissions, and viral publicity sign-ups. You should also get them on your Twitter, MySpace and Facebook pages.

6. Expansion

Expansion should occur organically but as a passive mechanism. You should expand through acquisition and by merging various subdivisions of your company with other entities to exploit the scalability of that strategic partner.

7. Remain in View and Keep Your Name in the News

Stay in the public eye with traditional publicity channels such as TV, expert panels, and providing free information. Make yourself available to give interviews if something is happening within your industry. You should also have a publicist who's constantly pitching you to the media.

CHAPTER 7

MAKING YOUR STOCK GROW FAST

Eight factors exist that will allow your stock to flourish, especially in the current economic environment.

1. SOLID CORPORATE INFRASTRUCTURE

Establish a solid corporate infrastructure that's conducive to domestic and international expansion. This infrastructure should also allow for product and service diversification.

2. WELL-PEDIGREED C-LEVEL EXECUTIVES

A well-pedigreed C-level executive staff should be able to demonstrate a proven track record of helping companies flourish when they are in situations similar to yours.

3. GROWTH THROUGH ACQUISITIONS

Public companies typically cannot grow organically so you need to publicize potential acquisitions, even if they don't go through. The hype alone can really increase your share price and will often introduce your company to potential investors.

4. STRATEGIC PARTNERSHIPS

Strategic alliances are extremely important. Global and domestic strategic partnerships can help you break into other markets by aiding with your product diversification. These partners may have localized legislative contacts and distribution channels you can use to expand.

5. VIRAL PUBLICITY CAMPAIGN

A viral publicity campaign can take advantage of social networking sites such as MySpace, Facebook and LinkedIn. They may also include how-to videos, unique article submissions and press releases. You can also blog about authoritative solutions for industry problems.

6. EXPERT PANEL POSITION IN MEDIA

The CEO and other key leaders of the company should talk about your industry by appearing on expert panels on radio or television. A crawl at the bottom of the TV screen or frequent radio announcements should provide the leader's name, title, company name, and trading symbol. These programs reach their audience very quickly, so you need to

make as many appearances as possible to inform potential investors that you have begun public trading. Public appearances allow your company's experts to demonstrate their knowledge to a broad audience without the need to purchase advertising time. People are more receptive to objective news and talk programs than ads.

7. WHITE HAT EMAIL AND NEWSLETTER ANNOUNCEMENTS

White hat email and newsletter announcements allow you to simply keep in touch with potential investors, since you won't be promoting your stock with these methods. The mailings will have company and contact information, so you should always be prepared to field phone calls from people who are interested in getting more information about your company. Prepare a package that you can mail through the U.S. Postal Service as well as email attachments.

8. MARKET MAKER AND BROKER ACTIVITY

A few employees in your company should do nothing but communicate with market makers and brokers to encourage them to look at your stock. This strategy will keep these people informed on your company and could convince them to sell your stock. They won't be calling businesses and soliciting them as is the case with a boiler room operation, which is the kiss of death for any public company. You'll just be calling businesses to provide good information that can help them decide if they want to buy or pitch your stock.

9. GROWING WITH ACQUISITIONS

Many entrepreneurs and executives want to move forward with going public merely for the purpose of raising capital through the sale of stock. They usually don't consider the strategies needed to maintain the momentum, such as the amount of equity to give up initially and the amount of equity to sell over time.

Business professionals may also fail to consider the need to capitalize on the use of securities as collateral for loans and lines of credit.

Putting securities up as temporary collateral for loans and using them to grow through the acquisition of strategic alliances is one of the most profound strategies that companies use. This strategy allows companies to retain equity while capitalizing on their public entity.

Entrepreneurs should view stock as cash and designate it for appropriate purchasing strategies. Stock that is monetized through collateralized lending can be highly effective so long as the exit strategy is secure. Your attorney should be familiar with this activity and able to audit the contract for aspects that could strip the stock transaction of its advantageous nature.

Debt that converts to equity means you'll give up a portion of your bargaining leverage for future transactions, so you shouldn't surrender equity unless it is necessary. Many companies will lend you money against your securities without having to give up long-term equity. Use this strategy wisely to ensure you never have difficulty obtaining capital. Avoid predatory pump-and-dump scams!

The use of stock to purchase strategic partners is more relevant today than it has been in the past. Purchasing a company with stock that can be monetized over time is a highly effective means of growing a business through acquisition. Going public on the OTCBB is also a quick and easy way to begin using the many methods of capitalization with a public entity. Going public merely to raise capital with your market maker or broker is selling yourself short. Take advantage of the ways in which your securities can work for you.

CHAPTER 8

HOW TO SUCCEED WITH A PUBLIC SHELL MERGER

CORPORATE INFRASTRUCTURE

Some companies create a public shell corporation with which to go public. It can be registered and ready to go as soon as a company merges with it. A shell company has shareholders but minimal to no assets. Your company may also purchase a public shell that has already met the regulatory and other legal requirements that public companies must obtain. This strategy will eliminate many of the IPO steps that a company normally must perform to go public.

Ensure your company is a successful corporate entity with the following five elements before you merge it into a shell:

1. C-Level Executive Pedigrees

Your C-level executives such as CEOs, CFOs and COOs will need solid pedigrees.

2. Viable Business Model

A viable business model is necessary for an adequate shell. Most companies with shells charge a modest upfront fee, but they will take the majority of their fee on the back end. This strategy typically requires the business to already be running and turning a profit.

3. Domestic Strategic Alliances

You'll need solid domestic strategic alliances to provide your business with adequate growth potential.

4. Online Viral Presence

You'll also need a solid online viral presence that uses all the typical online media such as video, press releases, unique article submissions, social and news bookmarking. You'll need to maintain your own blog, and you should also be a contributing writer to other industry blogs.

5. Traditional Publicity

Brand yourself and your C-level executives as well as your individual products and services. Wrap these brands within the corporate name and abbreviation. You can also obtain traditional corporate publicity through radio interviews and industry periodicals. Expert panels on television, local news and national news are also effective methods for obtaining publicity for your company.

WHAT TO WATCH OUT FOR WHEN BUYING SHELLS

You need to look out for a few items when buying shells.

AVOID PINK SHEETS

Legitimate companies do not invest in pink sheets to buy shells. Stay away from pink sheets as they do not provide any benefits. Traditional accredited investors are very reluctant to invest in pink sheets, whether they are institutional investors or private equity investors.

CHECK FOR LIENS

Perform an in-depth check for liens before buying a shell.

FREE TRADING SHARES

Beware of free trading shares, even when the board members of the shell don't mention them.

PUMP AND DUMP

Avoid buying a shell from a pump-and-dump company. These companies will have shell holders and a solid investor-relations strategy for the first 90 days after your company goes public. The shell holders will sell all of their shares after that point, leaving you with a shell that has only a fraction of the value that it should have.

ANGRY SHAREHOLDER LIQUIDATION

Use caution to ensure you don't buy a shell from angry shareholders who are attempting to liquidate their corporation. These business entities can't succeed in the public arena, since the shareholders will be suing the shell. These lawsuits can be easily transferred to your business.

POST-PUBLIC NEEDS

You'll need four basic elements to thrive after your company goes public.

1. Strong Investor Relations

You need a strong, ongoing investor-relations campaign, not just for the first 90 days, but for six to twelve months after the company goes public. It will just be maintenance after this period.

2. Scalable Exit Strategy for Investors

You'll need a scalable exit strategy that will allow investors to sell their investment without this affecting your share price significantly. You'll also need a way for the initial seed capital investor to cash out without damaging your share price.

3. Daily Trading Volume and PIPE Financing

Your new public entity should trade at least 50,000 shares per day to ensure you have solid funding sources available for PIPE financing and other institutional securities-based financing. Even traditional accredited investors will often issue loans based on securities at a low loan-to-value ratio.

4. Growth via Acquisition

Focus on growing your company through acquisition after it goes public.

CHAPTER 9

GLOBAL EXPANSION

CORPORATE INFRASTRUCTURE

Your current corporate infrastructure is the first factor you must deal with when attempting to expand globally within a short time and on a massive scale. We'll use China as a sample target market in this chapter.

C-LEVEL EXECUTIVE PEDIGREE

Your C-level executives need to have an established record in dealing globally. Crossing national borders is a completely different type of transaction than dealing domestically.

SCALABLE CORPORATE CONCEPTS

Your business concept must be scalable, since service-oriented companies typically work best for an expedient expansion into the Asian marketplace.

DOMESTIC STRATEGIC ALLIANCES

You should have your domestic strategic alliances in place before going public. This approach ensures you have a domestic support base already in place if you find a solid strategic partner in China. You'll then be in position to become a one-stop for your Asian partners since you'll be able to help them with any needs they face with their expansion ambitions.

ONLINE VIRAL PRESENCE

Companies from Asian countries such as China, Korea, Japan, Malaysia and Indonesia typically maintain a U.S. or Western European presence in the form of an office or at least an attorney. This allows these companies to perform due diligence on potential strategic partners, which typically begins with a Google search on the company, product line, services and any potential liens on your corporate entity. It's therefore imperative that you keep a solid online presence that includes videos, social networks, articles and press releases. These online formats should provide public information regarding the company such as events, services and products.

EXPERT PANEL-WORTHY PR

Many investors review podcasts and videos of your company executives when making an investment decision. Create audio and video interviews of your leaders that show them as industry experts, and place them on your blog or website. This strategy is an essential element if you wish to go global.

EXPANSION PROCESS

Know your target market, including its culture, economics and politics wherever you decide to expand.

IS YOUR SERVICE NEEDED IN CHINA?

Do you offer a service that is needed in the Chinese market? Most American or Western European products cannot be sold in China due to the currency difference, although services may be in high demand. For example, the Chinese government is putting $85 billion on clean energy, alternative energy and cleaning up urban water systems. You can therefore compete for contracts if you offer an engineering service with PhDs on staff. This is the perfect type of service to bring into China.

DISTRIBUTION ALLIANCES

You certainly don't want distribution to impede your strategic alliance with a partner in Asia who wants to take on your services and promote them to its client base. Establish alliances for distribution to your target international market.

LOCAL AND FEDERAL SUPPORT

You also need solid alliances with agencies or officials at all levels of the U.S. government, including the federal, state and local levels. Foreign companies will be impressed when they see the names of senators, governors and members of

Congress on your letterhead, vouching for your services and efforts.

DIFFERENCES IN BUSINESS ETHICS AND PRACTICES

Be prepared for the differences in business ethics and practices in other countries. For example, businesses in China fully expect payoff or bribe money, even though it's illegal. You must how you'll proceed when you're confronted with that type of thing. You'll also encounter this issue in other Asian countries, Eastern Europe and India.

EVALUATING STRATEGIC PARTNERS

Companies keep three separate books of financial records when you perform your evaluation of potential strategic partners. They use one book for their annual taxes and another to lobby companies like yours for strategic partnerships. The third financial book is the in-house accounting records, which show accurate figures. You need to access this book if you want to know the correct numbers regarding the company's performance.

LOCAL RESEARCH CONTACTS

You should have a local handler when creating mergers, acquisitions and strategic global alliances. This is someone with solid contacts in local and federal government, as well as the local business scene. You'll certainly need a local handler if you wish to establish a business presence in Shanghai, Hong Kong, Beijing or smaller cities in China.

PLUG-IN BUSINESS MODELS

The difference in currency between the U.S. dollar and Chinese currency is increasing at a minimum rate of 10 percent a year. This difference allows you to take off on the global sales of your products or services if they cater to the Chinese market.

Chinese companies often feel more comfortable in dealing with a public entity or a company that is in its pre-IPO stages. Stock in these companies may be traded on the OTCBB, AMEX, New York Stock Exchange or NASDAQ. The Bulletin Board is a platform that qualifies for recognition and legitimacy in China.

Chinese companies typically want to go public, usually through the OTCBB. Assist these companies with the desire and ambition to go public on a U.S. platform. You can usually get them to qualify for the OTCBB if your accounting firm has a forensic top to your accounting firm. Put their financial records together to help them achieve this goal.

CHAPTER 10

ADVANCED CORPORATE STRATEGIES

WINNING IS TEMPORARY, ANNIHILATION IS PERMANENT: CORPORATE STRATEGISTS SPEAK

You have probably hired a strategies consultant to help you gain a much-needed edge over your competitors if you're a board member or C-level executive. This is especially likely if you're in a cutthroat industry such as the pharmaceutical, biotech, technology, and software industries

Your consultant will help you realize that winning is only temporary, and it is only a matter of time before that competitor is stronger than ever, once again posing a major threat to your organization. You must continually fight to keep your economic position in your niche marketplace.

You won't stop a mugger by kicking him in the shin if he is coming at you with a knife. You'll want to grab a steel pipe and smack him over the skull until he's lying on the ground. A chump lying unconscious on the ground ceases to be a threat, and business is no different.

The key to lasting victory is to annihilate the opponent, although you cannot do this directly. Several indirect ways exist for obliterating a competitor to the point of no return.

Feed your opponent's more aggressive competitors with devastating information that you've acquired on your opponent. This information should cause damage in a way that offers no rebound potential. Obtain information about the weaknesses of your opponent's C-level executives, board members, advisory board members, product or services. Provide angry customers with a public platform upon which to voice their anger. Step in, be invisible and use your social media agent to make these guys rock stars.

You should evaluate your competitor's share price when bad press is crippling them. Buy some stock and dump it after checking with your attorney about any legal issues regarding this strategy. Repeat this action with any major competitor.

MANY WILL STRIVE BUT FEW WILL SUCCEED IN ACHIEVING A POWER POSITION

Corporate and political strategies are similar in many ways since the ultimate goal of both is to achieve recognition for making a contribution to economic growth. This is the one power tool that transcends all other contributors to power. The entity that gains traction regardless of any economic disaster surrounding will deliver on promises of jobs and capital to a targeted geography or economy.

The person who gains a following for the ability to step into a position of power and swim in shallow, shark-infested waters will be attacked from all angles. It is therefore crucial for such a person to eliminate the factors that facilitate these attacks. The ability to make a massive statement such as this requires natural genius as well as knowledge. It is a fact that the eyes are the most sensitive part of a shark's anatomy. Surfers and divers who remain calm when a shark is circling before an attack will immediately attack the eyes of the shark with anything that is available such as a kick, punch, fingernails or a knife. An executive who dives into a realm as competitive as obtaining the upper hand in a general corporate or political power grab must make a similar effort.

Don't waste time on aspects of competition that won't have an immediate, devastating attack on your competitor. A punch to the tail or fin won't do anything in a shark attack, so rip out the eyes and pummel the eye sockets. The shark will be blind to your position even if it continues to attack, which eliminates its position as a threat.

Study your competitors. Identify their past affiliations and determine what they were like in the past. Dig up dirt on your competitors but don't discuss it directly as this will make the source of the negative press too obvious. Use a third party, commonly known as a cat's paw, to deliver the bad news. A cat's paw should be completely unaffiliated with you or your company, and you should issue the information via unaffiliated messengers to ensure they don't realize they're being used by you.

Identify your target's vulnerabilities. Is it voting record? Pump and dump schemes with other public companies? Are they lapdogs to the political establishment? To which candidates are they contributing campaign money? Who has the CEO elected as CFO or COO, and is there any blatant demonstration of misjudgment?

A group of 100 lost travelers in the desert will seize every possible advantage and fight as dirty as they have to in order to win if you offer an ice cold bottle of water to them. This is what happens during a power grab.

Bring a steel pipe to fist fight, not a slinky to a fist fight; bring a steel pipe. Don't go to war with paper airplanes and silly putty. Use remote-controlled drones that will be able to inflict massive damage from a distance. Don't enter into a power grab without the backing of adequate support and influential names, as the results could be disastrous.

USING WAR STRATEGIES TO ELIMINATE COMPETITION

You can adapt the art of war to our economic environment. How does a new regional military power or upstart guerrilla troop solidify its position? Their leaders identify their adversaries and eliminate them.

How is business competition any different? These strategies are identical, although the actual elimination process differs. War is fought with bombs and guns, while economics is fought by eliminating a belief system that perpetuates the money behind a company. Remove the belief system upon which the company is based and you eliminate that company's ability to survive.

The purpose of promotions such as corporate branding and marketing center is to influence the minds of consumers to create an emotional need for your service or product. The few purchase decisions that are spontaneous are based on the consumer's perception that a product or service is available in combination with the threat of losing that product or service.

The best kind of idea to inject into the mind of an involuntary recipient is like a candy-coated treat, as opposed to a spinal tap. It should be smooth and easy instead of painful and forced. Some sugar coatings are presented in the form of a comedic TV commercial where laughter is the mechanism that is used to bypass critical faculties, while a sappy emotional segment may work for others.

The key to obtaining and maintaining one's position in an industry is to identify your immediate competition and deal with them. Move on to the next potential threat after you have eliminated each one.

An elimination strategy that tends to work for the immediate competitor regardless of industry is to analyze the regional market and find a company of equal size who is in direct competition with you. Identify his local competitors and strategically align your agenda with their promotional tactics via a third party. Help them to pinpoint and weaken specific products and services of your competitor without their knowledge. The second phase of this strategy is to introduce yourself through a third party and buy equities in these companies. Contractually obligate them to use this capital for designated promotional solutions that will grow your company. Use this money to flood the region with your products and services, and instruct your new partners to contact their established customer base with mailers, phone calls and in-person sales calls. Use these opportunities to introduce your company and its solutions to these customers. This strategy will cause your competitor to lose traction, and their stock will begin to fall, assuming it's a public company.

Buy stock in this competing company but not enough to increase the share price. The combination of multiple subsidiary elements attacking your competitor along with your firm's purchase of equity will cause the share price to fall, providing you with the control you need in order to remove your competitor as an obstacle to your growth.

Aid the process of your competitor losing market share by implementing a sell/buy strategy after consulting with your attorney for legal advice. This will cause your competitor's share price to reach a critical volume, allowing you to step in and flood the market with the stock that you purchased previously. This strategy can send your competitor into the penny stock domain, which is the kiss of death for any company that wants to survive and eventually qualify for the NASDAQ. View the stock purchases as gaining long-term market share rather than losing money.

Step in as the savior with investment capital, an acquisition proposal or a subsidiary merger once your competitor is close to shutting its doors. The company will be so weak at this point that it will have no choice but to accept one of these options. This regional strategy will allow you to eliminate a competitor while creating a virtual monopoly. It is a template strategy that is effective in a variety of political and economic situations, although you may need to customize it for specific circumstances.

COMPETITION CONTROL AND DECONSTRUCTION

I'm typically brought into a public company or large private corporation as a structuring consultant, or fixer. The company is usually in the middle of a crisis management situation, and my firm analyzes the problem, looks at it from multiple angles, applies various processes and finds a solution to solve the problem at hand. It sounds easy, but it isn't.

A hostile takeover or slander situation often begins with the firing of an employee or an overly competitive bid for a large contract. Both situations have the same indicators, so the C-level executive in charge needs to identify the problem before it becomes an out-of-control publicity nightmare or takeover situation.

It is crucial to identify the individuals at the root of the problem and defuse the situation before it explodes. Most of the problems that your company will face are employees who are in your office right now. They could be an overzealous sales manager who believes he has the intellectual capability to run your company better than you can. Promote him if he's right, but test him first. Offer him a severance package and explain his non-compete agreement clearly if he's wrong.

Scare the life out of him when he is terminated by ordering security to walk him through the legal actions that will occur if he makes any attempt to reveal your secrets or defames your firm in any way. Bring in your corporate attorney to do the same. The CEO can then come in as the nice guy and ask him to accept his severance package and find a job that will meet all his professional and emotional needs.

Other potential issues with employees include one who seems to have something counterproductive to say about everything. This may include the manager with a bad case of the grass-is-greener syndrome or executives who are too entrepreneurial.

You need a protocol in place that will allow you to take a proactive approach in countering negative PR if a situation does become public. You should have a media specialist on call who remains informed on your corporate strategies and proprietary processes. He should be ready to counter defamation and other virtual crimes by quickly posting on a blog. This strategy can help protect your company's reputation.

At least 90 percent of your company's problems will come from those who are currently employees. Evaluate your executives who have access to trade secrets or issues that could damage your reputation. Show your staff how you handle dissension by finding someone with the potential for creating trouble and make an example of that individual. Make your response known to the staff and you'll find that most potential issues can be eliminated down before they arise.

DO YOU HAVE A CORPORATE PLAYBOOK?

A football team has an offensive and a defensive playbook. The offense studies plays that will strategically position the team to score. The defense puts plays together that reduce the opposition's ability to score. Defensive plays also include ways to gain possession of the ball and run with it.

These sports strategies are also applicable to business, economics and politics, but you need a playbook. Common scenarios where a playbook is most helpful include a consultant being hired by a regional government to put strategies in place to turn the economy around, where the adversary is the lack of jobs and funds. Other examples include a corporation that treats its competition as an adversary, such that the corporation puts strategies in place to counter their competition's market position. A politician who puts a scheme together to crush the campaign of a rival who threatens his position also needs a playbook for his strategy.

A playbook is a series of schematics that visually break down the offensive and defensive measures that will enable you to gain an edge over the competitor. It will allow you to gain more control over public opinion, marketability and other aspects of your position. These plays should act as templates that can be plugged into different scenarios, complete with contact information for clearly-defined associates. These scenarios include strategic alliances that can offer a scalable offensive, media contacts to help get a story into the media and situations that adversely affect a competitor.

Don't try to do this on your own. Hire a seasoned tactician to ensure you don't wind up in an unrecoverable situation.

ANALYZING BODY LANGUAGE AND MICRO-EXPRESSIONS

I find myself seeking out concepts that will give me an edge over the individual across the table as I've grown in my career as a strategies adviser. I'm sometimes brought in for negotiations, but I may also be hired to put a BOD together or to qualify a new CEO for a public company. Sometimes I need to take companies public or help them grow through acquisitions and mergers. You can't survive in my small, incestuous industry if you can't perform and deliver results. Strategies consultants are often brought in for a turnaround strategy and there is no room for error, so I need a diverse bag of expert techniques. This will allow me to choose various pieces and assemble them together into a customized puzzle.

Reading micro-expressions and body language are some of the most critical elements I was fortunate enough to harness early on. I was first introduced to this concept on my flight home from an assignment in Germany. The guy sitting next to me was an interrogator and his skill was incredible. He traveled around the world teaching government and military organizations how to read micro-expressions and full body language. This allows a skilled observer to determine if an individual is lying, excited, nervous or sad. I immediately saw the applications for business, and he gave me some guidance on a few key concepts during the long trip back. I feverishly scribbled them down as fast as I could, and he gave me the titles of some great books to read for further study.

I use these concepts every day, and I suggest micro-expression and body language training to any executive who makes decisions affecting the future of a company and people's jobs. This training allows you to notice many things about a client's body language when you talk to him, such as his walk, shoulder placement and back position. You'll also notice details in his expression that indicate his mood such as the crease marks on his face, and the position of his mouth and eyelids. Your attention should then shift to the intonation of his voice, choice of vocabulary, arm position and foot position. Is his hand covering his mouth as he talks? Where are his eyes looking when he's talking to me? Use trigger questions to activate these micro-expressions, so you can evaluate his feelings and control the conversation.

APPLYING COMPETITIVE PRESSURE POINTS

I remember seeing a chart of pressure points in the human body on an executive's office in Asia. This gentleman had an interest in martial arts and acupuncture, and talked for an hour about these subjects. I naturally began thinking of the economic and business applications of pressure points as he was talking. Apply pressure to one particular area of a competitor's company structure and the entire entity squeals in pain. Apply pressure to the distribution of an organization and the clients cancel their contracts. Offer free services and clients no longer need to pay your competitor for those solutions. Find out if the executive VP has a drug problem, get proof and make this information available to the public via a third-party loudmouth.

The body falls back into its regular functional state once the pressure is released from a pressure point, but it's still sore and the natural instinct is to nurse that particular area. You can apply multiple simultaneous pressure points to the injured limb, creating an opportunity you can exploit.

Traditional competition in the United States is vicious. You should create a "body chart" of your closest competitor's business model before applying any pressure. Each sensitive area such as the fingers, limbs, jugular vein, toes and kneecaps should be labeled with an aspect of the company's business. Assign crucial elements to each aspect such as executive weakness, distribution platform, vital vendor relationships and other crucial elements.

Chart your approach to apply pressure only when it's needed. Step away from your CEO position and clean the toilets if this sounds too sadistic. The objective is to weaken your competitors to the point that they are no longer a threat, not to put them out of business. Make all of your actions indirectly through the actions of another party.

It usually requires only a modest whisper about a weak point in the body of a corporation and regional competitors will create their own opportunities from there. You'll barely need to lift a finger, and you can orchestrate the whole thing from the treadmill in your office. You can also apply this strategy to political scenarios. Run these scenarios by your attorney before moving forward.

DO YOU HAVE THE 'IT' FACTOR?

Hollywood calls it the "it" factor, but the rest of us call it "presence." It's that thing you can't put your finger, but successful people have it and the rest of us want it. But what is it? Defining this invisible quality is like trying to nail jelly to the wall but let me give it a shot.

The "it" factor that makes a person a magnet is a combination of elements such as facial expressions, verbal communication and body language. High-level executives try to acquire a fluid combination of these factors to create an identity that stands out. This identity is consistent, yet virtually impossible to quantify and mimic.

I personally know executives who spend many hours standing in front of a full-length mirror and practicing their responses to different scenarios. They create muscle memory so they can physically express a particular mode and hold it. I don't mean standing still like a statue. I mean that successful people practice remaining in a posture throughout a hypothetical conversation until it looks natural. This posture reflects the message they want to convey to clients, investors, competitors or others. They have a confidence routine with an "I care" look and posture. We've all seen politicians and interviewers use this look that includes the head slightly tilted, a gentle nod, eyes tenderly squinting, shoulders rounded and spine bent just so. There you have it, the "I care" look.

The "it" factor doesn't come naturally to anyone, no matter what people tell you. However, you can make it seem completely natural and effortless with practice.

CHAPTER 11

WHAT EVERY BUSINESS PLAN MUST HAVE

It's no mystery that companies are having a difficult time obtaining funding with the legions of template-loving business-plan copycats currently polluting the web. It used to be that when a company was ready to get down to business for serious expansion, they would call a consultant who would help them bring all the pieces together in a strategic fashion. The consultant would then author a business plan using his extended industry knowledge in combination with the unique concepts of the client's business.

This business plan would include everything that venture capital firms, angel investors, private investors and institutional lenders would need in order to make a quick, no-nonsense decision about whether to fund the company and the amount of equity they would receive in return.

Predatory consultants seek out start-up business prey and put them through a costly obstacle course and house of mirrors. They reel in their prey with a few big words and industry terms, but they are going to put your business plan together with template software. This software will spit out overly generalized business plans that receive laughs and snickers before investors and venture capital firm toss the business plan in the trash. This treatment leaves businesses too broke and exhausted to move forward with their expansion plans using a solid consultant.

Call a consultant who is completely submerged in the venture capital industry and has experience with plugging businesses into the capital machine if you want a real business plan. A qualified consultant will meet with you so he can assist with any corporate structuring or turnaround issues that require attention before implementing the business plan.

You'll need to do one more thing after filling the company's structure with executives, management, strategic partners, advisory board and a BOD. You must select the mechanism to use for raising capital. Are you seeking debt, equity investment or both? How much equity will you give away for the amount of cash you're seeking? How many shares does your corporation currently have and so on? You'll probably need to generate a PPM or take your company public on the OTCBB. Implement the business plan after you have completed these steps.

Don't shoot yourself in the foot by authoring the business plan on your own. Your consultant should include the following topics in the business plan:

Executive summary with objectives

Company overview including company position, company vision, key successes, technical achievements, commercial position and technology

Platform

Business model

Strategic analysis

Market analysis

Five Forces analysis

Barriers to market entry

PEST analysis

SWOT analysis

Process development map

Management team

Products and services

Competition

Financial model and projections

CHAPTER 12

INVESTOR RELATIONS, CRISIS MANAGEMENT AND CORPORATE PUBLICITY: PROPAGANDA WARFARE

The old adage "Any publicity is good publicity" isn't true in business. This concept is sometimes taught by college professors, but it was disastrous for a client of mine. Executives have emotional intelligence and real-world experience, while a professor's knowledge may be limited to academia.

The turbulent world of investor relations encompasses crisis management and corporate publicity. The fluctuations in this niche profession require emotional stamina, and are not for the faint of heart. The ability to parlay a crisis situation into one that stimulates trading is a gift that not everyone possesses.

I know successful IR consultants who received As and Bs at a state university, sold cell phones the year after college, got their Series 7 certification and traded successfully for a few years. They made a good income but got bored and left the industry, only to re-enter on the stock promotions side. These IR consultants have the technical experience needed to evaluate a stock and test it for vulnerabilities. They also have the industry contacts and street smarts needed to promote the company in a manner conducive to superior public interest and investor comfort.

Successful IR, PR and crisis management comes down to creating a template for information distribution. It then becomes a process of providing the content that will convince investors that the company will benefit them.

A company should have an abundance of positive information available to counter crisis management issues. It must always be ready to publish at least three positive responses for every negative report. This positive informant should take the form of a publicity template. What should your template look like? You need a combination of contacts for various media such as TV and radio, along with an ample supply of information sources with a large following such as blogs, article directories and podcasts. The publicity template should also include double opt-in email lists to investors, shareholders and legislative-style public relations specialists.

It's a fact of commerce that you're going to run into problems that could hinder your company stock or reputation. It is therefore important to implement crisis-management solutions and practice using them they are needed. Hire a crisis management consultant who can prepare your company to survive scenarios that would otherwise cause your company's demise. This consultant should be calm and even-keeled, with no nervous habits such as nail biting, sniffing and shuffling of feet. Watch out for candidates who drop names to impress you with their abilities through their association with another entity or individual. This type of consultant is unlikely to succeed since they will tend to abdicate responsibility.

Look for involuntary micro-expressions when interviewing a crisis management consultant. Ask a few control questions to which you know the answers and observe the facial reactions immediately after the question but before the verbal response. Then, ask questions that require critical thinking and observe the facial reactions again. Look for similarities among the control questions and test questions. You should be able to make good guesses as to whether the consultant is telling the truth, lying or exaggerating after you have discovered his "tells."

Ask the candidate to describe crisis-management scenarios he has encountered in the past, including the processes that were put in place to deliver a successful result for the client. Ask him to elaborate on his most powerful crisis management tactics. Determine what he has done on the IR side to generate trading volume and share price. Ask him how he would pump your product or service through his PR stratagem to achieve an optimal outcome.

Crisis management specialists should be more of a strategist than a general tactician. This means they are able to apply their knowledge to the current environment, good or bad, to obtain a desired result.

ESTABLISHING INFLUENCE

Tactical consulting is a raw and dirty business. Few people understand this small, elite group of experts and fewer still have mastered its concepts. CEOs and company executives in all industries should apply the concepts of tactical consultants.

Executives must understand the idea of power more than any other concept. A professional's ascension to positions of influence and power within an organization or industry power involves certain unbreakable laws. The following rules for corporate strategies consultants are prerequisites for the rise to power in the corporate world.

Corporate power is the exercise of economic influence and is driven by greed, self-confidence and the refusal accept anything but the top position within a specific industry. These individuals must possess the ability to customize and implement a solution that changes the fate of a dying company. They must be able to construct an infrastructure that perpetuates growth and stimulates longevity.

The ability of an individual to instill a no-holds-barred mentality within a capable executive group will save a company from becoming a statistic. The unrelenting passion to win and the tactical action of this executive will allow him to shoulder the burdens of the company and its employees. These characteristics are necessary for a leader deal with the stress that results from maintaining mission focus.

This individual will enter into battle and force the other side to surrender on his terms. He can break through bureaucracy and create multiple synergetic strategies to stimulate corporate growth. An executive who is primed for corporate power wears a velvet glove over an iron fist. He is quiet and calm, yet calculating in his demeanor. He can calmly step into a negotiation while assessing the vulnerabilities of everyone in the room, allowing him to press his agenda.

An effective corporate executive won't fall for offers of false friendship from potential competitors, but he will reciprocate to those showing true camaraderie while keeping them at a distance. He will always allow those around him enough rope to hang themselves if it will strengthen his company and his position within his industry. The executive who has mastered the art of power will be able to exploit the weaknesses of his opponents, then step back and watch them self-destruct. This strategy is more effective than risking repercussions by directly attacking an opponent.

Professionals who master these skills will find themselves in consulting positions where they are hated by their client's employees but loved by the shareholders. Add some of these characteristics to your repertoire and observe the response of those around you if you own a business or are in a senior position at a corporation. You'll find that you naturally develop a sphere of influence due to the effect of these characteristics on those around you.

You'll become a problem solver and the go-to person with a reputation for being able to structure any situation to your company's advantage. This reputation for being a real leader can earn you rapid promotions and a bidding war to retain your services.

INVESTOR RELATIONS SCAMMERS AND PUMP-AND-DUMP CHUMPS

You have probably experienced staggering swings in daily trading volume if you have a public or pre-public micro-cap company. These swings have various causes such as federal legislative announcements that affect your industry, failure to meet the previous quarter's financial projections and failure to keep the public informed on events within your company. This poor communication can cause your big stockholders to sell their shares, creating a ripple effect throughout your shareholder base.

The BOD and C-level executives will meet to develop strategies when your company finds itself experiencing minimal trading volume or share dumping. These typically include a number of short-term strategies that will produce a quick rebound and drop in share price in addition to strategies that will produce a long-term stimulation in the company's growth. Corporate executives will contract with a micro-cap promotional specialist when they decide to take a more aggressive approach to investor relations. This specialist will typically implement strategies to improve trading volume in the short term and distribute information to provide long-term benefits. These information sources may include press releases, C-level expert panel discussions, podcasts, blogs and industry journal interviews.

It's very difficult to know the good guys from the bad guys when a company seeks the expertise of a professional stock promotion firm for the first time. Executives are sometimes in such a rush to save their company that they will open conversations with consultants who represent the underbelly of the IR beast. Keep several important factors in mind when evaluating IR consultants.

Don't try to sound like you have all the answers. Do more listening than talking during the first few meetings, and hold these meetings in person if possible. Geography is important as most of the real players in IR are from the Northeast. Brokers who have lost their license often flee the borders of Manhattan and move to Tampa or Boca Raton to begin to sell IR services. I'm not saying that all the IR firms in Florida are scammers since I've used some brilliant strategists from that region. This generalization on geography is just an insider joke in the IR industry.

Look for certain body language, facial expressions and voice tones when meeting with these consultants. An IR strategist who is too relaxed is usually a poor choice. They are probably pump-and-dump artists if they aren't drilling you with questions about your corporate structure, future announcements, executive pedigree and other issues needed for a real campaign. Obtain proof of their track record by with dates and stock symbols for companies with which they've worked in the past six months. Track the performance of those companies' stocks. You are looking for a significant initial jump in the share price followed by a gradual increase and stabilization.

Here is a short cautionary tale of the stereotypical con artist you want to avoid. My office is strategically located in the Philadelphia area because we perform various types of consulting so I need to be reasonably close to Washington, D.C. and Manhattan. I typically stay in New York for a week or two when I am working on a BOD formation or C-level recruitment for pre-IPO companies. I work with the brokers and consultants via back-to-back meetings so we can get the job done in a reasonable time. I also meet with new contacts for additional services my clients need, such as investor relations during this time.

I got a call from an older gentleman during one consultation in New York. He saw my profile on LinkedIn and he introduced himself as an IR strategist with 25 years in the business. He said he had an incredible ability to help shareholders sell their stock into the marketplace without damaging the company or the stock price. He added that he could make it happen fast because of his large, current database of accredited stock investors. I had two or three clients who could use that service immediately so I agreed to meet him.

I noticed that he was around 80 years old when we met at my hotel. He had a fake tan, a disco-style shirt open to his navel and enough fake gold to make Mr. T blush. We went to an Italian restaurant attached to my hotel and we spoke. I had water, he ordered a meal and I got stuck with the check. Yes, it was as pathetic as it sounds. I wanted to remain objective even though this ancient relic and disco champion looked and sounded like a Doobie Brother with lockjaw and a serious vitamin D deficiency. I therefore invited him to attend a meeting later that week with a group of investors. I wanted to see if I was missing something, in case he was an eccentric genius. We universally agreed that this Doobie Brother was an idiot after the meeting, so we just passed over him. The kicker to this story is this joker billed us more than $8,000 for his consultation. I still get emails from this chump to this day.

Investigate every detail about an IR group before signing a contract. Never sign anything until you're absolutely comfortable with the terms. Use shares as collateral for payment when possible and negotiate aggressively if you're paying in cash.

CLAIMING GROUND: THE OFFENSIVE IN CORPORATE EXPANSION

Growing a company requires you to overcome countless obstacles such as a slow economy, minimal sales, lack of branding and a weak corporate structure. A company often hits a roadblock to growth when a competitor is too organized or strategically smart to leave any portion of the market unclaimed. It's sometimes best to throw in the towel and move on if you've waited too long to respond to a competitor's actions. The objective in these cases should to sow chaos and confusion in the path of the opposition.

The use of propaganda can affect the longevity of your corporate position by creating negative branding. It is therefore important to use this tactic only when necessary. Conduct your actions indirectly so that the public does not recognize your involvement in a propaganda campaign.

Local competitors in your market are typically the best choice for a cat's paw when you wish to paralyze certain aspects of your target's corporate model. You may wish to offer assistance to the most aggressive local competitors by marketing collateral that pursues the customer base of your target competitor. Offer better rates, better services or better terms to get clients thinking about their options. This strategy can defeat the seemingly organized retention model of your target. It will affect smaller competitors most easily, but this chaotic process is scalable to the extent that you can also use it for larger competitors.

Expect the target's infrastructure to begin coming apart at this point. Companies typically pass the blame when times get tough, which depletes the cohesive nature of an otherwise solid company. This is when you want to begin generating rumors and recruiting your competitor's key personnel. Start with the salesman and work up to the sales manager. Sales are the lifeblood of any organization since no sales means no revenue.

Recruit sales agents when possible. Hire a local executive recruiting firm to do this for you and instruct them to use aggressive tactics. You particularly want sales agents and all their contacts. Provide the executives who do not accept your offer with some negative gossip to take back to their company. This tactic can help weaken your target from within.

You should also pass the names sales executives who turn you down to your target's smaller local competitors. This will allow local competitors to take turns trying to recruit the sales executives from your target. The issue is not whether this effort is successful; the objective is to poison the target organization, rather than kill it. Increasing the restlessness of the target's key personnel will confuse its management.

Move to the financial side after sales. The financial department of an organization is critical to its success and these workers are often dissatisfied with their lot in life. Financial employees often blame their employers for this, making them prime targets for propaganda. Find out where they have drinks after work, buy them a round and become friends. Tell them that you'd like to hire them directly or find a job with one of their company's local competitors. This tactic will provide these employees with a false sense of confidence that only lasts as long as their relationship with you remains intact.

Continue these tactics as long as you can to slowly eliminate your largest competitor as a threat. This will allow you to step in and claim your rightful position in the marketplace. You may need to perform this process a few times to achieve an optimal effect, although it will always have an impact as long as you remain in control.

CORPORATE PUBLICITY AND THE NECESSARY ELEMENT OF EMOTION

Strong publicity is always necessary for branding, direct marketing and lead generation whether your organization is a small localized business or a large international corporation. Publicists in the past have sent pitch letters to radio shows, television news corporations and print media. These letters often provide some assistance to an otherwise dead publicity campaign.

The publicity profession has changed in the 21st century. It has merged with marketing to create a one-stop shop for a powerful, rapid-response form of promotion known as publicity marketing. These consultants offer cost-effective, guerilla marketing that includes everything a business needs in one turnkey solution. Publicity marketing typically includes direct response media campaigns, branding and other types of targeted promotion.

Publicity marketing has acquired a significant portion of the corporate promotion marketplace, forcing marketing to evolve. This is reminiscent of the changes during the 1960s that introduced the notion of emotions branding. A good publicity marketing company will infuse a marketing campaign with emotion to captivate the subconscious mind, where the most powerful images are stored. This strategy provides your company with brand identity in the mind of your customers.

The most experienced publicity marketers are able to induce sales by bypassing the customer's conscious mind, which performs judgment and critical thinking. These messages create emotional impact with the use of colors, terms and word positioning, which makes your brand synonymous with your industry in the customer's mind. The publicity must also present the consumer with a solution that creates a direct need for your service. You must demonstrate how your brand will solve a problem for the consumer, regardless of widget you're selling.

How is your brand going to pass through the critical faculty of the conscious mind and create a state of contentment in the consumer? Your product or service probably can't do this on its own, but a good publicity marketing company will know the approach that will allow it to fulfill your customer's emotional needs. This tactic will help ensure customer loyalty.

POWER AND THE PYRAMID OF INFLUENCE

I find it fascinating to stand back and watch people interact when I go to political functions or other gatherings that claim to have important people in attendance. Politicians and CEOs always stick to surface conversations, while upstarts look over the shoulder of their conversation partner for the opportunity to move on to someone with more influence. I can watch this interaction for hours and speculate with friends on where we believe someone is in his career.

One thing that supplicants often fail to realize is that their chosen conversation partner is often just a pawn to another more influential person. Upstarts typically choose to associate with the face of an organization grow their career and raise their social standing. However, someone with real power is usually exerting their influence on these puppets.

I have yet to find a true puppet master who is comfortable in the public eye. It is easier to step back and dictate the moves of pawns by using the upstarts' natural willingness to be controlled by their betters. Most people are content with the illusion of influence as long as they believe they are the source of that influence.

When I have a client who is in the process of globalizing, it is important to get their cause built into legislation. I never communicate with the politician directly, whether I'm in the USA or Europe. I contact the person who funds his campaign with capital and votes, instead of his traditional blockers such as his campaign manager or assistant. The process is usually easy from there. Politicians such as congressmen, governors and mayors of large cities are willing hand puppets who are chosen by special interest groups. The real purpose of these politicians is to ensure that votes are in place for the re-election, so long as the politician supports the special interest group's agenda.

Uninformed and uninitiated people usually believe that the apex of the pyramid of power is represented by the face of a political organization such as the Republican or Democratic political parties. Politicians are influenced by three powers, including money, lobbyists and special interest groups. Donating money to a politician rarely gets you more than a single favor such as a letter for your kid to get into private school. True power in politics is social influence and the ability to control a large number of voters. For example, it is rare to find a single conservative Republican politician in the South who isn't backed by the Southern Baptist Convention or Christian Coalition.

Business executives can also apply the principle of bringing votes to a particular cause. The primary objective of setting up strategic alliances and recruiting board members or CEOs is to obtain money and votes. We look for people who have successfully raised capital and increased revenues during their time with their previous companies. The "votes" in the corporate world are the strategic alliances that are formed by the executive. What does the candidate's direct contact portfolio look like? Whom will they bring through the door to offer an instant benefit for my client's company?

You don't actually need to have money if you are trying to establish yourself as a power broker in the political or corporate realm, just access to it. This access is the ability to directly parley with those who cut the checks and the influence to get them to do so when the time is right. Influence, alliances and voters are easy to obtain for those with a natural ability to network. Decide what you are trying to influence and build your network from there.

Don't start from scratch when you try to put together a group of followers. Lobby figureheads or management to begin brokering power among these groups. Make introductions, but ensure you omit enough information that people need to call you to accomplish something. You should be able to build a solid power base of influence from this point.

Don't come across as too eager; get to know these individuals in a calm, relaxed manner. Research them before you initiate contact and ensure your first contact doesn't seem too intentional. You may want to run into them at your local tennis club or golf club and strike up a conversation. Make a mental note of the topics that come up during the conversation, including their current needs. This information will tell you how to refer and network them with asking anything in return. Your objective at this point is merely to establish contact and affiliation. Build your sphere of influence in this way to rapidly achieve your goals without catering to the wrong people.

THE ROAD TO CORPORATE POWER

You could dominate the marketplace by being a nice guy in a perfect world. Executives could get to the apex of the power pyramid with kisses, hugs and backrubs. The unfortunate reality is that you achieve market domination by bringing fear and chaos into situations that call for it. Ascendance to the top of the business food chain requires you to step on the necks of others.

I try to listen to happy-go-lucky leadership training for points that will persuade me to think differently, but I am submersed in the ugly corporate world of political power plays. I have no choice but to look at things as they are. Corporate reality isn't the feel-good philosophy of a new age guru; it's Machiavelli and Nietzsche.

The world is an ugly place and the path to power is blocked by distractions and naysayers. Rich and powerful people haven't made a fortune by being Mr. Nice Guy. They earned their millions like Donald Trump, by inheriting.

You're probably beating down a path for your children if you're a first-generation C-level executive, so that all they have to do is pick up where you left off. You're making enemies, then tossing and turning at night to preserve a place for your children. Fortunes are built on the bodies of those who have given up the trek to prosperity. You must put on blinders and ear plugs, and then keep moving forward. Focus on immediate goals when you get discouraged, but keep your ultimate goal in sight. Study "The Prince" by Machiavelli, "The Art of War," "The Five Rings," "48 Laws of Power" and other books that will train you in the tactics you'll need to conduct economic warfare. This path has no room for a sidekick and those from whom you expect allegiance will almost certainly disappoint you. Your loyalty to them will probably prove counterproductive, so you may need to make some difficult decisions along the way.

CRISIS MANAGEMENT DONE PROPERLY

The following information isn't for economically naïve utopia seekers. If this describes you, press that X in the top right side of your computer screen, open up a new browser and go to some other website. Keep reading if you are more comfortable with the truth and understand that the apparent tranquility of corporate life is just an illusion.

Your competition's underhanded methods will continually bring a new crisis to a head. These methods will include blatant lies and sucker punches to harm your image or reduce your client base. Your response should be just as dirty and damaging. Never allow a competitor to get close enough to engage you and initiate an offensive if you can avoid it. Take a tap to the chin when necessary and respond with a sledgehammer to your opponent's skull. You'll need to conduct personal and professional attacks against your opponent from every angle. Good crisis management requires you to have a small militia ready for action at any time.

Your first response to a crisis should be to counteract the negative publicity against you or your company that has been issued by your opponent. Use all of your company's authority and reputation to call the information into question by publishing rebuttals to their claims. This will confuse the public and reduce your competitor's ability to follow through with their attack. Ensure that every source of information on your competitor's claim also contains your rebuttal.

Identify the individual who has taken it upon himself to publicize his negative opinion about your company. Who is his direct management? Who is the executive over this management? Who are the company's most obvious strategic partners? What is their most critical distribution or sales alliance? Is it a public or a private entity?

This information should allow you to create your plan for annihilation. It must be a quick, well-planned offensive that shows no mercy. Your counterattack must be handled by third parties and be as public as possible.

The best way to accomplish this is contacting local competitors who have been affected by your target's presence in their market. Organize them into a regional militia that will infiltrate your opponent and act on your behalf. Get them to attack by showing them the advantages of owning the regional market share of your target. Offer them economic incentives for their efforts. Use an outside social media vendor to help this militia gain a regional advantage against your target through the distribution of social media favorable to your cause. Maintain control of this social media distribution to ensure the release of this information is timed perfectly.

This attack must affect the individuals who initiated this action against your company. Challenge every aspect of their reputation to ensure they can't regain their position within the industry. Work your way up the management chain of these individuals, ensuring you mention their names at each stage.

Corporate crisis management is an offensive strategy, rather than a defensive action. Its intent is to annihilate your opponent in a swift, decisive and public manner. This response to a crisis serves to demonstrate the consequences of opposing you to other potential opponents.

CORPORATE DISINFORMATION AND THE ROAD-BLOCK CHAOS STRATEGY

Politicians and corporate executives both use the same "chaos injection" and "roadblock" strategies for disseminating disinformation. Both mechanisms involve control public opinion through indirect methods. This control is essential for guiding a group or individual along a desired path.

The implementation of these strategies to obtain a desired outcome requires you to create conditions that encourage people to take the path of least resistance, which is a natural human trait. Leaders establish control quickly and efficiently by appealing to the ego via subconscious triggers. They initially focus on two groups, including those who follow a particular brand of product and those who are dedicated to a particular religion. The primary reason for targeting these two groups is they are searching for an identity and a voice. They also want to gain the prestige that the brand has in their immediate environment. These groups tend to adopt a brand's cause in order to convince themselves of the legitimacy of their beliefs. Those who either don't wear designer brands or proclaim their religious beliefs are typically more self-assured and communication is less likely to bypass their subconscious critical faculties.

Creating a roadblock system is typically much easier than it seems. The United States government is a master of this method. For example, the "get out and vote" campaign makes the general population feel important by convincing them that their individual votes can change the course of a presidential election.

Media propaganda can implant post-hypnotic suggestions through methods such as Sunday sermons and activism to obtain a desirable outcome. For example, the government is gradually removing rights with the Patriot Act. Americans are giving away their constitutional rights with very little effective objection from either end of the political spectrum. Anyone who attempts to bring attention to this issue finds that a series of roadblocks has been set in place to reduce their legitimacy through media control. A corporation can execute the same strategy.

I've been offered many contracts to perform propaganda and crisis-management projects, but we are a boutique firm that only accepts projects that cater to our direct skill set. We therefore pay close attention to our potential client's industry niche, C-level pedigree and board organization. We also consider our potential client's objective. They are afraid to say it, but most of our potential clients want mind control over their customers, potential customers and shareholders. This is really what they want to achieve when they make statements like, "We need to get our information to the public in a way that is conducive to investor confidence and client satisfaction" or "we need a crisis-management template put together for this problem so that our stock doesn't plummet."

Our potential clients want to distribute an idea it in a way that enters the public's subconscious and is virtually impossible to remove. But how does this company get the public to accept this idea?

A majority of the population believes in the concept of free will, but the reality is that most choices are the direct result of a message by an outside source that views individuals as a target to control. The exercise of so-called free will is really just a path that leads the individual through a series of choices that are motivated by personal gain. The ultimate outcome has been determined by tacticians and strategists who have been following the individual's progress and encouraging the desired choices via media, religion, education and peer pressure.

You can apply this strategy to any business, political campaign or agenda. It's just a matter of having the proper support mechanism in place to influence individual choice.

CONTROLLING MOVEMENT IS THE BEGINNING OF CONTROLLING THE MIND

Control of the ego is the only true path to the objectivity needed by the professional executive. You must learn to dissociate the connection between emotions and the micro-expressions that are the direct result of subconscious responses. This control will enable you to conduct a meeting, interview or professional conversation without exhibiting the body language that will reveal your intentions. Body language and micro-expressions provide professional interrogators with information that allows them to control the conversation and its outcome.

These physical indicators are the primary means by which we conduct communication. The automatic facial expression that occurs before the response to a question is the second most relevant communication mechanism. A firm, confident expression and body posture will enforce your authority and keep the opposition guessing as they try to analyze the psychological intent behind your words. Adjust your body position and facial expression only when you are trying to use these actions to enunciate your verbal communication.

The third communication mechanism is the silence between the prompt and the response. The last person to break the silence will usually have the upper hand. The verbal component of communication is usually the least effective mechanism since it often prevents you from retaining the upper hand.

Verbal expression should be a combination of short yet powerful responses that emphasize command and authority over vocabulary. The art of intonation allows you to underline and emphasize key words that prompt your opponent's subconscious mind to absorb the ideas and concepts behind the words.

Think of a conversation as an opportunity to create posthypnotic cues in your target's mind that can be triggered in later conversations. Your body language, vocabulary and intonation allow you to plant an idea that will prompt your target to act in a certain manner when stimulated to do so.

Control over your environment is rather simple when you implement the above strategies and make them part of your communication in professional settings.

CARRY A BIG STICK? NO, CARRY A STEEL CLUB!

If you were walking into a group that was guaranteed to be hostile and you could choose one of the following as a weapon, which would you take: a rubber band, a Bible, a paper bag or a spiked steel club? If you took the rubber band, you could snap at the people who were trying to pummel you into a bloody pulp. If you took a Bible, you could pray for a miracle while the mob gave you a beating. You could put the paper bag over your head and walk around blindly until you got slaughtered.

I would grab the steel spiked club and swing it as quickly as possible to escape the mob with no injury to myself. Forget the big stick; you want to walk lightly and carry a steel club. Why should you treat your approach to crisis management any differently? You have competitors who spend their time thinking of ways to defeat you. You want the most effective crisis-management specialist available, one who is consumed with honing his skills. You don't want a specialist with minimal contacts to assist you in rebounding from an economic attack.

You need someone who can retaliate from an attack with greater force than your competitor can imagine. Use a multi-pronged attack by going after multiple targets, including your competitor's products, integrity, and reputation. Continue to attack your competitor until they beg for mercy and then put them out of their corporate misery. Publicize your actions to ensure the public knows why you took that company down.

Business is a form of warfare that is not for the faint of heart. Having the right specialists in publicity and crisis management on your side can make all the difference.

CORPORATE STRATEGIES: CHAOS WITH AN AGENDA

The corporate and political strategy of chaos is a world where puppet masters reign supreme and a misguided populace begs to be controlled. It is the flipside to conscious reality. I will explain.

The origin of man's nature lies within the confines of chaos where the concepts of leadership and subservience coexist in harmony due to the order within clearly defined positions. The principal leader is typically invisible and his subordinates voluntarily satisfy his subconscious need to be the head of an organization. The artificial fulfillment of this need perpetuates this process.

A common application of this perception is the manager in a corporation. He appears to at the apex of this structure to those below him, but the reality is that he is subservient to the vice presidents, who are under C-level executives. These executives are under the BOD, who is held liable to shareholders. This stratagem is only the beginning of order within chaos.

The shareholders are the group with the loudest voice in a corporate structure. They in turn are marionettes of the corporation, which completes the circle of influence. The interdependency of elements in this circle becomes clearer, when the third source of influence in this model is introduced.

This circle has an outside source of influence that is more powerful than the elements within the wheel. It is the agenda of those who capitalize on the perpetuating disarray that keeps those confined within the circle, unaware that they have the ability to be liberated. The agenda produces the ideas that enable this environment to exist. Without it, intellectual, scholastic and professional development would cease.

The true masters of this structure are an evolving collection of global alliances with diversified yet interdependent interests that perpetuate this universe. They include political leaders with a need to create jobs within a region and organizations attempting to capture a controlling majority of an industry. Each of these leaders is accountable to another structure within the socioeconomic hierarchy, which provides the stimulation needed to perpetuate this inter-reliant existence.

CRISIS CONSULTANTS

Imagine walking through the desert, malnourished and dying of thirst. The sun blisters your skin beneath layers of caked-on dirt and sweat. You're on your knees about to surrender to the elements, thinking that your situation couldn't possibly get any worse. Just then, you feel a powerful hand grip your hair and yank it back. A dull, rusty blade scrapes against your skull as the hair and skin are ripped from your head.

This is what it's like to be on the receiving end of a corporate crisis-management specialist. A rebound from this attack is impossible and defeat is imminent.

A crisis-management consultant can help you resolve your crises after board, strategic alliances, lawyers and priests have failed you. He should be intellectually capable, yet primitive in his fighting tactics. Crossing this consultant is economic suicide.

Only a few consultants provide services in this small niche and they are very expensive. You'll have typically exhausted all your resources fighting a disinformation campaign, hostile takeover attempt or defamation scheme against your firm when you finally recruit a crisis-management consultant of this caliber.

Individuals can be malicious but corporations can be even worse. You need a solution that is twice as devastating and shows no mercy to combat this tactical malevolence. Effective crisis-management strategists will have a briefcase full of charts and templates, the way your accountant has tax forms. They sit up at night running through various scenarios, with counterattacks that range from a general response to a full-blown attack intended to destroy your opponent.

A crisis-management consultant should have a full comprehension of your company's situation before they ever set foot in your office. They'll have already identified the source of defamation, the mechanism of the message distribution and the immediate partnerships that have assisted the opposition. They will also be able to predict the limits of their resources.

The first thing your crisis-management consultant should is to provide you with a list of new alliances. This list will typically include companies that are outside your direct contact capability and will require an introduction. The consultant will typically prepare these contacts beforehand so they are waiting for your call. He'll also provide you with pages of charts and timetables that will allow you to implement a strategy for your rebound.

The usual objective of this practice is to destroy your opposition's information-delivery, which will typically cut the jugular vein of your opposition's corporate lifeline. The next goal is to isolate this company, leaving it exposed to your counterattack. The purpose of this tactic is to polarize your opposition with industry disinformation implying that their current course of action is hazardous to the company's health.

The distortion of your opponent's distribution channel is the next step in your disinformation campaign. Social media and other high-volume information distribution channels is the typical mechanism for accomplishing this goal. Your opponent will soon be just another rotting corpse along your highway to success.

The company that initiated this dirty process to gain market share should be eliminated as a threat. It may survive as a business entity, but it will have much less influence within your marketplace. The strategist who implements this process thoroughly will allow you to begin serving your new clients, who once belonged to your opponent.

Your company should keep arsenal of strategies in place for the time that a crisis arises. This should include a list of targets that will eliminate the threat by creating disarray in your opponent's message-delivery system. Use the 3-to-1 rule, meaning that you'll counteract each negative statement with three positive responses. This tactic will create a massive amount of favorable publicity that will allow you to deal with the threat.

Reduce the possibility of a negative campaign gaining momentum against you by implementing a positive publicity campaign. Your IR team should put this in place on your behalf if your company is public. Every positive message about your company should be put through the following channels automatically: social media, press release, phone room, unique article submission, podcast, webinars and other free information sources. Distribute this positive information gradually so that it generates loyalty for your company, while remaining scalable and streamlined.

THE ROAD TO PUBLIC MARKETS

The road to achieving a trading symbol and successful trad-ing volume with the OTCBB, NASDAQ and NYSE is littered with the carcasses of companies just like yours. I don't say this to discourage you, but to help you approach this goal with caution. You'll need a consultant assisting you with this task. You'll be better off using a boutique consultant rather than a high-volume consultant. Boutique firms will perform the pre-public structuring of your company in a way that will get the ball rolling and build momentum that will allow you to steamroll through the IPO process. This will allow you to overcome the critical aspects of generating trading volume after you go public.

Your company will need a high trading volume to succeed in the public marketplace. A public company without trad-ing volume cannot hope to survive, regardless of the stock exchange. Consistent trading volume will allow a company to collateralize its securities for cash, lines of credit, loans, acquisitions, merger facilitation and just about anything else it needs, even if the trading volume is modest. Stock dilution can damage a company if it occurs too quickly, so it's impor-tant to dilute the stock gradually.

A candle burns out quickly when it's lit at both ends, so have your strategy team should create benchmarks that will create steady growth. Apply the Sun Tzu method of "slow, slow, quick, quick" to your business. To steal another con-cept from The Art of War, don't burn out your troops with constant warfare. Take time to step back, regroup and re-evaluate your options. You will probably need to adjust your current plan within two months. Each adjustment to your plan should trigger a series of responses as you inform alliances, employees, consultants and associated management down the chain of command.

Listen to your qualified consultants without becoming bureaucratic over minor decisions. Micro-management doesn't work and is one of the biggest reasons for corporate failure. Company founders need to know when to step back from their operations. Don't try to analyze and approve a process in which you have no background. Your ego can cripple the growth of what could be a prosperous company.

Your company may be able to grow despite your ego, unqualified staff and overly-involved founders for the first couple of years, but these factors will eventually eliminate your chances of expansion down the road. Qualified management, the absence of ego, strong alliances and a process that centers on scalability will take your company over the top and succeed in the global marketplace.

CHAPTER 13

THE ART OF EXECUTIVE INTERROGATION: HOW TO HIRE THE RIGHT EXECUTIVE EVERY TIME

Your hiring process should be clear, concise and deliberate. This should hold true whether you're taking your company public, expanding your corporation, performing an in-house cleanup or filling a C-level position at your company. You also need to consider every skill of the candidates you are interviewing in addition to their resumes and references. Pay close attention to what they say as well and don't say, in addition to their gestures, verbal intonations and overall presence. Here are a few details about what to look for when you hire an executive.

Evaluate the candidate's overall attire, including his or her suit, dress shirt or blouse, tie, jewelry dress shoes and even shoelaces. Are the suit, shirt and tie crisp, conservative and pressed? Are the shoes shined, scuff free and are the shoelaces in good condition? Observe the condition of the socks or stockings when the candidates cross their legs. These things may seem artificial, pretentious and pointless, but bear in mind that you are hiring the appearance of the individual as well as the mind. The condition and selection of clothing tell you a lot about the candidate's subconscious thoughts and mindset. Do they pay close attention to detail? Do they have a clean presence? These things are "tells" every time an executive stands before a client or panel.

The interview is the next stage in the hiring process, where you will evaluate the candidates' intellectual and emotional fitness. How much do they know about your company? The answer to this question will demonstrate the candidates' motivation to become part of the team and begin making a contribution. The strongest candidates will come into an interview ready to define their role and describe what they bring to the table in the form of contacts and intellectual capital.

Ask the candidates to tell you where they see the company in five years with themselves in a leadership position. Ask them to provide five to ten strategic alliances they have planned for the company and what that will contribute to the company's bottom line. What expansion experience do they have? Ask them to elaborate on the pros and cons of taking a company in your position public. Ask the candidates to critique the top executives of your company and describe how they would reorganize the company if they had their way. Go past their educational pedigrees and ask them about their professional pedigrees, including the manner in which it has prepared them to join your corporate team.

Pay close attention to the candidates' physical gestures and take notes. Look for subconscious movements that communicate their responses as you're asking them questions. Look for gestures that demonstrate confidence, arrogance and security. Are they sitting back in the chair when they are talking? A qualified executive should sit up straight without letting his back rest on the chair. You, on the other hand, should be relaxed and sitting back. Are their legs crossed? Are they using their hands when they talk? Is their forehead crinkled or relaxed? Do they have a strong vocabulary that can strengthen their presentation?

Hiring the proper executive for a specific role within the company can be challenging, but the right hiring process will help you weed through the poor choices in your search for the ideal candidate.

CHAPTER 14

PRE-IPO INVESTING: THE UNRIVALED PROFIT CENTER WITH MINIMAL ACCESS

A pre-IPO investment is a once-in-a-lifetime opportunity that always seems to happen to someone else. Everyone seems to know a story about an investor got in on an IPO for a software company and became a millionaire overnight. Another story like this is the one about a biotech IPO that had the closest thing to a cure for Alzheimer's disease. The company made a small pre-IPO raise and closed out the offering, again making the investors instant millionaires.

Are the investors who grabbed these opportunities exceptional in terms of their research capabilities and investment banking contacts that give them insider information? They probably did two simple things the right way. First, they made themselves available for opportunity by subscribing to IPO alerts from reputable firms. You could find yourself in the middle of an obscenely profitable venture if you're quick to act. Second, investors who are willing to take an acceptable risk may have the opportunity for a big reward. Forex, pink sheet pump-and-dumps and pie-in-the-sky concepts are obviously blatant risks that don't have a reasonable chance of paying off. These schemes are for millionaire adrenalin addicts who thrive off of the rush of gambling.

What is your next move if you get the rare opportunity to invest in a pre-IPO offering? Whom do you call to help you with research, and how do you evaluate this company quickly based on a typical PPM? It's fine to get a second opinion, but you still need to know what to look for in a pre-IPO investment.

The following steps will allow you to perform a spot audit on a company to assess its suitability for investment during the pre-IPO phase:

1. Look for a solid corporate structure consisting of well-pedigreed professionals in C-level positions. The company should also have a strong, diversified inter-industry BOD, a secondary advisory board and strategic alliances. The mechanism for distributing and sharing equity should be well-organized and compliant with SEC regulations. The share price should be based on a solid valuation by a reputable firm.

2. Is the firm in a growth industry? When you look at the founders' resumes in the business plan, are they serial entrepreneurs with a track record of modest success but minimal focus? Have they targeted their careers in a single direction? You want professionals who have worked their entire lives honing their skills and pedigree for this particular industry and opportunity. These qualifications will ensure in the founders will minimize the possibility that this pre-IPO company is a pump-and-dump operation.

3. What is the company's 12-month strategy after it going public? What is the growth strategy? They're in for a surprise if they think they can grow organically. They have to show a plan for post-public growth through acquisition and subsidiary merger. What subsidiaries have they have lined up and what will they bring to the company that will increase the value of your investment? What is their post-public market creation strategy and who is their IR firm? What is the IR firm's track record for dealing with companies within this industry? What is their globalization strategy for rapid well-controlled growth? Who handles their legal matters?

4. Are the company's founders politically connected? What strategies are they using to gain political and legislative support? What legislative bills are they supporting and what legislators are sponsoring the bill? What type of press and photo opportunities are the founders setting up to make their company the face of the industry?

Never invest in a pre-IPO with borrowed funds or capital that you need for any reason. Only invest with capital you're not afraid to lose, which goes for any investment. An investment in a pre-IPO can be very rewarding for the informed, accredited investor. Do your research and join the right circles of influence to obtain inside information on the company. Surround yourself with industry insiders and ask many questions.

CHAPTER 15

FINAL WORDS OF ADVICE: THE CEO IS THE NEW GOVERNOR

The objective of today's CEO is survival in terms of enterprise position. The CEO must pick up the remnants of the company that were left behind by the failures of its former executives. Today's senior executive needs to be a congressman, judge, mayor and priest all rolled up into one. The livelihood of the company's employees depends on the CEO's expansion tactics, emotional stamina, intellectual foresight and willingness to enter into an economic cage fight to protect the company.

Surround yourself with the most experienced advisers you can find as you expand and go public. Recruit guerilla networking specialists to establish strategic alliances to grow into new areas. Expand when your competitors aren't expecting you to do so. Stay in touch with shareholders by communicating with newsletters, email, and press releases. Participate in expert panel interviews on TV and radio.

Take your position at the apex of the power pyramid in your industry by demonstrating your expert status with podcasts, iPad information applications, webinars and blogs. Give the market free information such as how-to videos and detailed articles. Educate the public and lead them to your company.

Be a media mogul. If Migos can make great vids for cheap, so should an IPO co.

Promise low and deliver high to ensure you exceed the expectations of your customers and shareholders.

Leaders and followers exist in every environment, and each leader has a flock. Do your research and initiate communication with these shepherds. Show them the advantages of forming a partnership with you and everything else will take care of itself. Win-win relationships always yield possibilities for capitalization.

Seek out board or advisory positions with entities within your industry and establish powerful alliances where you can obtain publicity and distribution channels. Become acquainted with your legislative representation. Find out what bills they are sponsoring, and offer expert input and cooperation for legislation that is favorable to your industry. Publicize your relationships with legislators or your participation in a bill. Become the face of a movement.

Get involved with charity work at the grassroots level and change people's lives. Volunteer at a soup kitchen, offer a company scholarship to help hard-working seniors go to college, or coordinate with your employees to volunteer at nonprofit events. Publish this information through your regular channels to set the standard for philanthropy in your location and industry.

People no longer believe in their governmental leaders, including senators, governors, presidents and prime ministers. These positions are filled by power enthusiasts who accomplish little, which provides C-level executives and opportunity to step forward. This road will be a challenge to navigate, but these times require leaders who see the bigger picture and are willing to carry the torch.

Made in the USA
San Bernardino, CA
23 February 2015